MUSIC

This book belongs to:

D1343097

female voice

The female voice extends in a variety of ranges and tone colours, depending on the individual singer. The highest range of voice is called **soprano**. The middle range of voice is called **mezzo-soprano**. The lowest range is called either **contralto**, or **alto** for short.

I-Spy 5 for each ☐☐☐

male voice

The male voice, like the female, is classified according to its range. The lowest kind of voice is called **bass**. The middle range of the male voice is called **baritone**. The highest normal range is called **tenor**, but men can also sing in a higher 'falsetto' range, which is practised today most often in rock music.

I-Spy 5 for each ☐☐☐

a capella

a capella describes any music consisting only of voices, without any instrumental accompaniment. The word *capella* means 'chapel' in Italian, and it was used originally to describe church music, which was usually performed without any instruments in the Middle Ages.

I-Spy for 15 ☐

barbershop quartet

A barbershop quartet consists of four men singing together, each with a separate musical part. In earlier centuries customers in barbers' shops might play music as they waited to have their hair cut, and the barbers themselves would sing. More recently, the term has applied to a particular popular style of music.

I-Spy for 30 ☐

church choir

Church music is usually sung in four parts: soprano, alto, tenor and bass (abbreviated SATB). Nowadays women usually sing the upper two parts but, before the nineteenth century, they were not allowed, and boys had to sing instead (girls were completely excluded). Most cathedral choirs continue this older tradition.

I-Spy for **10** □

orchestral chorus

The orchestral chorus became popular in the nineteenth century to supplement the instruments of the orchestra. Unlike church music, men and women have always been welcome to sing in these kinds of secular groups.

I-Spy for **25** □

opera

Opera consists of soloists, and sometimes a chorus, who act out a musical drama with the accompaniment of an orchestra. Opera first became popular 400 years ago in Italy and has been an important category of music ever since.

I-Spy for **10** □

scat

Scat singing is a kind of improvisation used in some kinds of jazz, especially in fast 'be-bop' songs. The singer does not use real words, but invents a tune with made-up syllables and words.

I-Spy for **30** □

grand piano

The grand piano is the biggest and heaviest instrument you can find, except for church organs. The largest kinds of 'concert grand' are well over 9 feet (2.75 m) long. The earliest pianos were made by the Italian Cristofori about 400 years ago. They were much smaller and looked more like harpsichords.

I-Spy for 5 ☐

upright piano

Invented in 1800, the upright piano is a smaller and cheaper alternative to most grand pianos. Because the strings are vertical and not horizontal, it fits more easily into the home.

I-Spy for 5 ☐

player piano

In a player piano (also known as a 'pianola'), a special device is put into an upright piano which enables pieces to be played automatically. Pieces are coded on to a paper roll which has holes in it corresponding to certain notes. When it is started the keys are depressed as if by an invisible ghost!

I-Spy for 50 ☐

church organ

The church organ is the largest kind of instrument ever built, and it is nicknamed the 'king' of instruments. Several keyboards (called 'manuals') and a pedalboard are connected to pipes. These produce a sound when bellows force air through them, in the same way as a woodwind instrument.

I-Spy for **10** ☐

accordion

The accordion is like a tiny organ which is held in the hands. One hand controls a little keyboard and the other is used to work the bellows, forcing air past metal reeds which vibrate to produce sound.

I-Spy for **20** ☐

harpsichord

The harpsichord was the most common keyboard instrument to be used until the late eighteenth century, when the piano began to replace it. Unlike the piano the strings are plucked by goose quills. Harpsichords have one or two manuals, and sometimes they have knobs you can pull to change the quality of the sound.

I-Spy for **20** ☐

spinet

The spinet is a small, triangular kind of harpsichord, which was suitable for use by amateur music lovers in the home. The strings run diagonally or at rightangles to the keys, unlike those of the harpsichord (which are positioned more like the strings of a grand piano).

I-Spy for **30** ☐

tuning hammer

Most keyboard instruments must be tuned at regular intervals with a tuning lever (*bottom*) or tuning hammer (*top*). A piano must be tuned once or twice a year, but you have to tune the harpsichord almost every day!
I-Spy for **15** ☐

adjustable bench

Because people come in a variety of shapes and sizes, an adjustable bench is helpful to position you at the right height to play.
I-Spy for **10** ☐

pedals

The piano has two or three pedals. The right one is called the **damper pedal** and it allows all the strings to vibrate, not just the ones connected to the keys which are held down by the fingers. The left pedal is called the *una corda* or **soft pedal** and it produces a softer tone. The **middle pedal** (if the piano has one) can serve different functions.
I-Spy **5** *for each* ☐ ☐ ☐

violin

The violin (*left*) is the highest-pitched member of the violin family, which also includes the viola and cello. It has been used in folk music and jazz as well as in classical music. As with all instruments of the violin family, children can play on smaller versions of the adult instrument, to help smaller fingers and hands.
I-Spy for 5 ☐

viola

The viola (*below*) is the second highest-pitched member (or alto member) of the violin family. It is unique among orchestral instruments in that a violist's music is usually written in alto clef. Like all members of the violin family, the neck of the viola has no frets.
I-Spy for 10 ☐

cello

The cello (*left*), whose name is a shortened version of 'violoncello', is the lowest-pitched member of the violin family. Unlike the violin and viola, the cello is too big to be held and played against the neck, so you will see cellists rest the instrument between their knees. A sharp pin holds the instrument off the ground. Like all members of the violin family, the cello's strings are tuned at intervals of a fifth (five notes apart on the keyboard).
I-Spy for 5 ☐

double bass

Although the double bass looks like a larger version of the cello, it is not even a member of the violin family! The tuning system is based on intervals of a fourth (four notes apart on the keyboard). This is why it is, in fact, a member of the viol family. The double bass is used in the orchestra and in many jazz ensembles.
I-Spy for **5** ☐

viol

This is a viol da gamba, one of the members of the viol family. Viols were commonly used until the middle of the eighteenth century, when the violin family became increasingly popular. Ladies were not supposed to play string instruments at all, only to sing or to play a keyboard instrument!
I-Spy for **30** ☐

viola d'amore

The viola d'amore, which means 'viol of love', is the most glamorous instrument of the viol family. Unlike members of the violin family, which all have four strings, this instrument has considerably more. Some instruments have more than 20 strings, though not all of these are bowed.
I-Spy for **50** ☐

modern bow
The modern bow (*left*) consists of a concave piece of wood which holds tight strands of horse hair. Resin is rubbed on the hair. This causes the modern instrument's metal strings to vibrate (thus producing sound) when the bow is drawn across the strings. Bows are used most commonly to play members of the violin and viol families.
I-Spy for **5**   ☐

Baroque bow
The Baroque bow (*above*) differs from the modern bow most obviously in that the wood forms a convex shape against the hair. This makes the player use a different bowing technique. The modern bow began to replace it in the early nineteenth century.
I-Spy for **25**   ☐

classical guitar
The classical guitar (*left*) is a versatile instrument which has been used in folk music, blues, ethnic music, as well as in classical music. It has six strings and is plucked with the right hand, using either a plectrum or with the fingers alone. The left hand controls the pitch of the strings.
I-Spy for **5**   ☐

ukulele

The ukulele is a small kind of guitar with only four strings, invented in Portugal. It is particularly popular today in Hawaii, where the playing technique is distinguished by quick strumming.

I-Spy for 20 ☐

banjo

The banjo might look quite similar to the guitar, but there are many important differences. For example, the body is made of a metal hoop with animal skin stretched over the top, and there can be between four and nine strings. You can hear the banjo most often in American folk music.

I-Spy for 20 ☐

plectrum

A plectrum is a small piece of bone or plastic which is used to pluck the strings of an instrument. Some kinds are held between the thumb and index finger; others can be attached to the fingers alone.

I-Spy for 5 ☐

fret

A fret is a piece of metal (similar to a wire) which is attached to the neck of some string instruments at right-angles to the strings. It is used to help the musician play in tune. You can find frets on instruments as diverse as guitars, viols, and sitars.

I-Spy for 5 ☐

lute

Lute is a term used to describe a whole family of string instruments which originated thousands of years ago. The rounded backs of these instruments distinguish them from members of the guitar family, which have flat backs.

I-Spy for **25**   ☐

mandolin

Invented in Italy, the mandolin is a small member of the lute family. It has long been used for informal music making, and is today most frequently heard in ethnic or folk music.

I-Spy for **20**   ☐

sitar

The sitar is one of the most important string instruments used in Indian music. It has up to seven plucked strings as well as up to ten other strings (called 'sympathetic strings') which increase the resonance. Performers such as Ravi Shankar have introduced it to audiences across the world.

I-Spy for **50**   ☐

11

piccolo

The piccolo is the smallest and highest-pitched member of the flute family. Its piercing tone quality makes it suitable as an instrument in military bands as well as the orchestra. The body can be made of either wood or metal.

I-Spy for **10** ☐

flute

The flute is the principal member of a family of instruments which all share the same method of producing sound. The player blows across a hole near one end of the instrument and tone is generated in the same manner as when you blow across the top of a bottle.

I-Spy for **5** ☐

clarinet

The clarinet and other members of its family are recognized by their cylindrical wooden shape and the use of a single reed. The two most common examples are the Clarinet in B flat and the Clarinet in A. Before 1843 it was essential for a clarinettist to have both instruments, because limited technology prevented either single one from playing all the notes in every key. It is used in classical music, jazz, and ethnic music.

I-Spy for **5** ☐

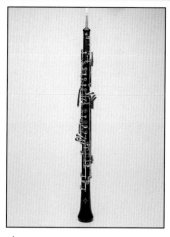

oboe

The oboe has descended from an ancient family of instruments originating in the days of the Egyptian pharaohs. It is distinguished by a double reed and a pear-shaped bell (the end of the instrument held away from the player). Today it is used as a member of the orchestra, and it produces a rich, if sometimes nasal, tone.

I-Spy for 5 ☐

English horn

Also known as the 'cor anglais' (French for 'English horn'), the English horn is not a horn at all, but a larger member of the oboe family. Neither is it English in origin: it was invented in Italy in 1760. Romantic composers, especially, have taken advantage of its beautiful tone as an orchestral instrument.

I-Spy for 15 ☐

bassoon

The bassoon and its relative the **contrabassoon** are the largest and lowest-pitched members of the oboe family. The wooden tube has to be so long that the instrument doubles back on itself like a hairpin, the sound emerging at the top of the instrument rather than the bottom.

I-Spy 10 for each ☐ ☐

13

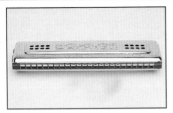

harmonica

The harmonica, or mouth organ, is a popular instrument for amateur music making because it is so versatile and cheap. The player blows along the side of the instrument which has many holes, each connected to a metal reed. It is especially popular in folk music.
I-Spy for 5 ☐

kazoo

One of the simplest instruments, the kazoo produces sound in the same manner as a comb and paper. You can sing or hum into it.
I-Spy for 5 ☐

saxophone

Even though the saxophone is made of brass, it is a woodwind instrument because the player blows into a mouthpiece which contains a single reed. There is a whole family of saxophones, ranging from the **soprano sax** (which is similar in size and shape to a clarinet) to the huge **bass** and **baritone saxophones**. The most common instruments are the S-shaped **alto** and **tenor** instruments, which have been especially successful in jazz and other popular music.
I-Spy 5 for each ☐☐☐☐☐

recorder

The recorder produces sound in a manner not entirely unrelated to the flute, because no reed is required to produce tone. The **descant** (soprano) instrument is particularly popular with children, but other members of this family of instruments exist, including the tiny **sopranino** and larger **alto**, **tenor**, and **bass** versions. It was invented in the Middle Ages or earlier.

I-Spy **5** for each   ☐☐☐☐☐

bagpipe

Although the bagpipe is today known especially as a Scottish instrument, its origins lie probably in Africa or Asia thousands of years ago. The piper plays a melody and a 'drone' note provides a basic fixed harmony. The bag (called the 'reservoir') is filled with compressed air, which makes it possible not to break the flow of sound when the player takes a breath.

I-Spy for **15**   ☐

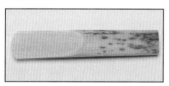

single reed

This is a single reed from a clarinet. The reed vibrates (causing sound) when the player forces his/her breath past it and into the mouthpiece. Other instruments to use single reeds include the saxophone.

I-Spy for **5**   ☐

double reed

This is a double reed from an oboe, similar to all reeds of the oboe family. The two reeds are tied together with a space in the middle for the player's breath to pass into the body of the instrument. The flowing air causes the reeds to vibrate, generating tone.

I-Spy for **5**   ☐

baton

Most instrumental conductors use a baton to clarify the movements of the hand and arm. The first conductor to use a baton was the composer Jean-Baptiste Lully (1632–87), who used a large staff to beat time. If an ensemble has no conductor, the first violin can use his/her bow like a baton.

I-Spy for **5** ☐

metronome

A metronome beats time automatically, either with a pendulum or with an electronic pulse. You set the tempo to a certain number of beats per minute. The metronome is helpful to find the appropriate tempo for a piece of music, and, as an exercise, it can help students to play in strict time.

I-Spy for **10** ☐

serpent

This strange-looking instrument earned the name 'serpent' because of its resemblance to a snake. It mixes characteristics of brass and woodwind instruments. The tone is produced in the manner of a brass instrument (the player vibrates the lips) but the finger technique is like a woodwind instrument (the player covers holes in the tubing). It was used most frequently in the seventeenth and eighteenth centuries.

I-Spy for **50** ☐

trumpet

The trumpet is a versatile, bright-sounding brass instrument used in orchestras, bands, and all kinds of popular music. Today, it has three valves, which enable the musician to play all the notes of the scale, and its curved shape makes it easy to hold. In medieval times, there were no valves and the tubing was long and straight: taller than the musicians themselves!

I-Spy for **5** □

valve

There are two kinds of valve which are used on brass instruments: piston and rotary valves. Both kinds fulfil the same function. When depressed by the finger, a valve redirects the player's breath through extra tubing. This causes the pitch of the note to be lowered. Valves make it possible for brass instruments to play all the notes of the scale.

I-Spy for **5**

□

cornet

Similar to the trumpet, the cornet is slightly shorter and it produces a less brilliant tone. Today it is not used in the orchestra, but you can find it in military and brass bands as well as in jazz.

I-Spy for **10** □

bugle

The bugle is probably the simplest of all brass instruments. Because it lacks valves, it is capable of playing only a limited number of notes. It was used to give signals while hunting or in battle. In the army it is still used for ceremonies.

I-Spy for **10** □

17

flugelhorn

The flugelhorn (German name *Flügelhorn* meaning 'wing horn') has a wider tube (or 'bore') than the trumpet and cornet, and this helps it to produce a warm, velvety tone. It is found most commonly in brass bands, but it is sometimes used in jazz as well.

I-Spy for **15** ☐

French horn – valved

The modern valved French horn has been used since the middle of the nineteenth century. It has a wider and lower range than the trumpet, and it produces a warmer tone. Notice that the player must rest the instrument in the lap because it is too bulky to hold like a trumpet.

I-Spy for **5** ☐

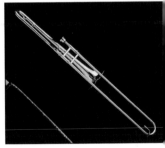

French horn – natural

Like the bugle, the natural French horn lacks valves. This means it cannot produce all the notes of the scale. Players compensate for this by placing the hand in the bell of the instrument, changing the pitch slightly. Also like the bugle, the natural horn has ancient origins in the military and in hunting.

I-Spy for **15** ☐

trombone – slide

The trombone is usually constructed like this one, with a slide that the player moves in and out. As a result, it can produce a *glissando* if the player wants (the pitch rises or falls continuously, rather than from one specific note to another). The trombone is used in classical music all kinds of bands, and in jazz.

I-Spy for **5** ☐

trombone – valve

The valve trombone was devised in the nineteenth century for use in military and brass bands. It is much easier to march with, and you don't have to stretch your arm to play all the notes. It does not produce such a pure tone as the slide instrument, however.
I-Spy for 15 □

tuba

The tuba is the largest and lowest-pitched brass instrument. It is so big that it must be played vertically, resting in the player's lap.
I-Spy for 10 □

sousaphone

The sousaphone was invented by American bandmaster John Philip Sousa as a replacement for the tuba in his band. It is held looped over the player's shoulder and it is therefore easier to carry in marching bands.
I-Spy for 20 □

mutes

Various mutes are used by brass players to alter the tone quality and reduce the volume of their instruments. All are fitted into or over the bell of the instrument.

Traditional mutes include **straight** (*bottom right*), **cup** (*centre top and bottom*), and **Harmon** ('wah-wah') (*top left*) mutes, as well as less conventional devices which are used especially in jazz, such as a **felt hat** and a **bathroom plunger**. *Top right:* bucket mute or Velvetone; *bottom left:* E.T. (extended tin) mute.
I-Spy 10 for each □□□□
□

drum set

There is no fixed arrangement for the drums in a drum set, but you will usually see a bass drum, snare drum, and two or more tom-toms, as well as a crash cymbal, ride cymbal, and high-hat cymbal. Drum sets are used particularly in jazz and rock.

I-Spy for 5

timpani

Among the largest of drums, timpani (or 'kettle drums') are usually found in the orchestra in groups of two or more. Unlike most drums in Western music, they are tuned to a specific pitch, and a pedal on the instrument can further vary the pitch.

I-Spy for 10

bass drum

The orchestral bass drum is considerably larger than that found in drum sets. It rests on its side on a stand, and it is struck by a large felt-tipped drumstick.

I-Spy for 5

snare drum

The snare drum produces its distinctive sound as a result of metallic strings (called a 'snare') which are tied across one of the instrument's two skin surfaces. When the drum is struck the strings buzz briefly, causing a sharp 'crack'! The snare can be disconnected if necessary, and the drum then produces a more hollow tone.

I-Spy for 5 ☐

cymbals

Cymbals come in a variety of sizes. Large orchestral cymbals are held one in each hand. The player crashes them together, not like clapping your hands, but rather in a sweeping motion with one arm moving up and the other moving down. Cymbals in jazz and rock are mostly suspended individually from a metal stand and struck with drumsticks.

I-Spy for 5 ☐

castanets

Castanets are used most often in Spanish folk music. They consist of small pieces of wood tied to a finger and thumb of one hand. The player, who is traditionally also a dancer, snaps the castanets together, producing a 'clicking' sound.

I-Spy for 20 ☐

triangle

The triangle is one of the simplest of all instruments. It is struck with a metal stick and it makes a tinkling sound.

I-Spy for 10 ☐

xylophone

The xylophone consists of a series of tuned wooden bars which are arranged to look like a keyboard. You strike the instrument with mallets. The xylophone originates in ancient times, when it was used by tribes in Africa and south-east Asia.

I-Spy for **10** ☐

tubular bells

Although they do not look like traditional bells, tubular bells ring like normally shaped ones. They are usually used as part of an orchestral percussion section.

I-Spy for **15** ☐

wood blocks

Wood blocks are struck by hard-tipped drumsticks, and they produce a hard, hollow sound. Note the slots in the blocks, which help to increase resonance.

I-Spy for **10** ☐

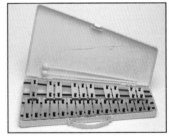

Glockenspiel

The Glockenspiel (which means 'play of bells' in German) consists of a series of tuned metal bars which are organized to look like a keyboard. They are struck with small hammers and sound like very high-pitched bells.

I-Spy for **10** ☐

celesta

The celesta creates a sound not unlike a Glockenspiel, but the player's fingers are used to play a keyboard which causes the metal bars to be struck.
I-Spy for 25 ☐

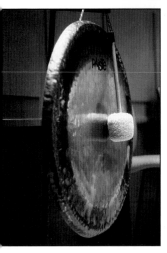

gong

The gong originated in ancient China and consists of a large round sheet of metal which is struck by a felt-tipped mallet. It creates a huge crash and is occasionally used in the orchestra, usually to mark special musical climaxes.
I-Spy for 15 ☐

bongo drums

Bongo drums always come in pairs tied together, and they are played with only the hands, without sticks. They originated in Cuba and are constructed by cutting out solid blocks of wood.
I-Spy for 15 ☐

congo drums

Congo drums are considerably larger than bongo drums, but are also played with just the hands. Be careful not to confuse the names! They originated in Africa and, like bongo drums, are used mostly in jazz and ethnic music.

I-Spy for 15 ☐

tabla

The tabla is the traditional drum of Indian music. There are two drums, one producing a high pitch and the other a low pitch. The player uses them together to make rhythmic patterns, striking them with only the fingers or the palm of the hand.

I-Spy for 25 ☐

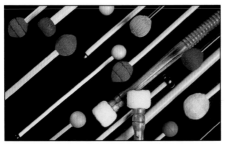

drumsticks

Drumsticks come in a variety of sizes, and the tips are usually made of wood or felt. All these differences contribute to the unique sound of the particular drum.

I-Spy for 5 ☐

synthesizer – analog

A synthesizer is any instrument that generates tone from electricity. It is called an 'analog synthesizer' if computers are not involved in the process. These kinds of machines have existed since the beginning of the century, but perhaps the most famous instruments are those built by Robert Moog since the 1960s.

*I-Spy for **10*** ☐

synthesizer – digital

Digital synthesizers have come to replace older, bulkier analog synthesizers since the early 1980s. Computer (digital) technology is used to create different kinds of sound waves.

*I-Spy for **10*** ☐

MIDI

MIDI stands for 'Musical Instrument Digital Interface'. It allows different pieces of digital musical equipment to work together.

*I-Spy for **10*** ☐

electric organ

The electric organ is a kind of analog synthesizer which was invented by Hammond in 1934. Its most characteristic feature is the intense kind of vibrato it can produce. Electric organs are associated most closely with jazz and rock of the late 1960s and 1970s.

*I-Spy for **10*** ☐

25

electric piano

The electric piano is not a synthesizer because real, physical vibrations are the source of tone, produced when hammers strike small metal bars inside the instrument. Electricity is used only to amplify these vibrations. You can hear the electric piano in popular music of the 1970s.
I-Spy for **15** ☐

electric guitar

The electric guitar differs from its acoustic classical relative most obviously in the method of amplification. In a classical guitar the vibrations are amplified naturally in the body of the instrument. In an electric guitar tiny microphones sense the strings' vibrations and send them to an electronic amplifier.
I-Spy for **5** ☐

electric bass

The electric bass is much smaller than its acoustic relative, the double bass. In fact, it is hardly bigger than the electric guitar! This instrument has four strings like the double bass and uses the same method of amplification as an electric guitar.
I-Spy for **5** ☐

electric drums

An electric drum does not need the kind of large cylindrical body you see on acoustic drums. Instead, small sensors are attached to the hitting surface. These send vibrations to an electronic amplifier away from the drum.
I-Spy for **15** ☐

symphony orchestra

The symphony orchestra consists of a conductor and four sections: string, woodwind, brass, and percussion. The exact size of the orchestra is determined by the composer! A **chamber orchestra** is a smaller version of the symphony orchestra.

I-Spy **5** for each □□

string orchestra

A string orchestra consists of only a string section. This includes violins, violas, cellos, and double basses. Sometimes a conductor is not needed and the musicians follow the leader of the first violin section.

I-Spy for **10** □

military band

A military band is an ensemble made up of woodwind, brass, and percussion sections. Although the armed forces use such bands, civilians can form them as well! Military bands often march in parades.

I-Spy for **10** □

brass band

A brass band is made up from a selection of brass instruments. Brass bands are particularly popular in the north of England, where they are often formed by employees of an industrial firm.

I-Spy for **10** □

INSTRUMENTAL COMBINATIONS

string quartet
The string quartet is one of the most successful ensembles in chamber music. There are two violins, one viola and a cello. The greatest composers of the quartet are Haydn, Mozart, Beethoven, and the twentieth-century composer Bartók.
I-Spy for **5** ☐

piano trio
A piano trio is a chamber music ensemble consisting of violin, cello, and piano. The combination of keyboard and strings allows the composer a lot of possibilities in the way he or she puts the music together.
I-Spy for **5** ☐

duo
A duo is an ensemble consisting of two musicians. Many different instrumental combinations are possible, but usually one of the parts is written for the piano (often as an accompaniment).
I-Spy for **5** ☐

soloist
A soloist can either be a person who performs music written for one person or a person who performs a highlighted part in music written for more than one player. The piano is probably the greatest solo instrument because it can play both the melody and harmony at the same time.
I-Spy for **5** ☐

jazz combo

There is no fixed group of instruments for a jazz combo (combination), but you can expect to find a rhythm section (which might include piano, bass, drums, and guitar) and one or two other parts: perhaps a saxophone, trumpet, or singer.

I-Spy for 5 ☐

big band

Big bands are large ensembles which play jazz. They were especially popular in the 1940s. They consist of a rhythm section, saxophone section, trumpet and trombone sections, and sometimes a singer.

I-Spy for 10 ☐

rock group

There is no fixed instrumental combination for a rock group, but most groups are made up of three or more players who usually sing as well. You will find at least a drummer, bassist, and guitarist.

I-Spy for 5 ☐

stage

This is where an orchestra or other ensemble plays. In opera and ballet it is where the drama takes place. In orchestral music it is sometimes necessary to raise the back part of the stage to help the musicians see the conductor.

I-Spy for **5** ☐

pit

A pit is where the orchestra sits in opera and ballet. It is a sunken area in front of and below the stage which allows the audience to see over the heads of the musicians and on to the stage.

I-Spy for **10** ☐

podium

In orchestral music, many conductors stand on a raised platform called a podium, which is found at the front of the stage. This helps the musicians to see him or her.

I-Spy for **5** ☐

organ pipes

In some concert halls you will see the pipes of an organ, and possibly the console where the organist sits. This is because some halls were designed for organ recitals. It also helps certain large orchestral works which call for the use of an organ.

I-Spy for **10** ☐

orchestra seats
Orchestra (or 'parterre') seats are those on the ground level in front of the stage. If you're not sitting near the front, it is sometimes best to take a coat to sit on, in case someone tall is sitting in front of you!
I-Spy for 5 ☐

balcony
Most concert halls have seats on at least one balcony. Some have up to three or four, and they might be named 'dress circle' or 'upper circle' as well. Often the best acoustics in the house are heard from the balcony.
I-Spy for 5 ☐

box seats
The most expensive seats in a concert hall are the box seats, usually found on the first balcony.
I-Spy for 10 ☐
Double for a Royal Box

green room

The green room is backstage where the soloist or other musicians stay before a concert and during the interval. Even though most green rooms are not painted this colour, green is considered the most relaxing colour for a nervous performer.

I-Spy for **10** ☐

acoustical fittings

Many concert halls are fitted with devices to help produce clear acoustics. In older halls you might see a large tapestry, which absorbs sounds and prevents echoes. More recently, specially designed panels made from various materials have been used instead.

I-Spy for **5** ☐

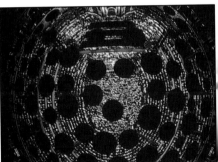

hanging microphones

If you look carefully you might see microphones suspended from wires above the stage and orchestra seats. These are often a permanent feature of concerts halls, used for recording performances.

I-Spy for **10** ☐

concert hall

You can listen to all kinds of classical music in a concert hall, from solo recitals to performances by symphony orchestras and religious choral works such as Handel's *Messiah*. Concerts of jazz or ethnic music are also sometimes held here.
I-Spy for 5 ☐

opera house

The essential characteristic of an opera house is that it provides a stage for the singers to act out the drama and a pit for the orchestra. Ballets also often take place in opera houses.
I-Spy for 10 ☐

stadium

Stadiums are able to provide far more seats for an audience than any concert hall. For this reason famous rock groups favour stadiums to accommodate their thousands of fans.
I-Spy for 10 ☐

park

You can find many different kinds of music in a park on a summer's day. You might hear buskers, radios, or a brass band in a bandstand.

I-Spy for **5** ☐

50 *for a concert from a famous opera singer*

street

A busker is a street musician who might play a guitar, harmonica, flute, or other instrument.

Occasionally you will find a group of buskers playing in an ensemble.

I-Spy for **5** ☐

music shop

Many music shops sell instruments as well as sheet music. Here customers might try out different instruments before choosing which one they want to buy or rent.

I-Spy for **5** ☐

cylinder

The oldest form of musical recording was the cylinder. Invented about 100 years ago, it was rotated by hand. A vibrating needle scratched the surface of the rotating cylinder, transferring the vibrations of sound on to a material which could be played back.

I-Spy for **50** ☐

gramophone

The oldest record players had to be wound up. Because this kind of gramophone was not electric, it had to rely on natural amplification. This meant that the grooves in the record made the needle vibrate, and these vibrations were naturally amplified in the large horn that you can see in the picture.

I-Spy for **25** ☐

electric record player

After World War II record players became cheaper and more popular. Advances in technology meant that the vibrations which were transferred into the needle were sent electronically to loudspeakers for amplification.

I-Spy for **5** ☐

cassette player

A cassette and cassette player offer a more compact alternative to a gramophone, especially as a portable **'Walkman'**.

I-Spy **5** *for each* ☐ ☐

CD player

The introduction of digital computer technology revolutionized the recording industry in the early 1980s. In a CD (Compact Disc) player a laser 'reads' digital numbers on the disc and a computer converts these into sound.

I-Spy for 5 ☐

DAT

DAT, which stands for Digital Audio Tape, has done for normal cassettes what the CD has done for records. Digital numbers are stored magnetically on tape and these are decoded by a computer into sound.

I-Spy for 10 ☐

amplifier

An amplifier is any device that magnifies sound. This can be done naturally, in the way that the bell of a horn strengthens the vibrations of sound. It can be done electronically, using a loudspeaker. An amplifier is also the part of your stereo system that contains the volume control, which boosts the electronic signal before sending it to a loudspeaker.

I-Spy for 5 ☐

loudspeaker

A loudspeaker is simply an electronic version of what happens on all musical instruments, to amplify the sound. Electric 'vibrations' (or pulses) from your stereo are connected to a magnet on the loudspeaker, which then starts to vibrate physically, causing sound.

I-Spy for 5 ☐

headphones
Headphones are tiny loudspeakers, which allow you to keep your music to yourself. Be careful when you wear them outside: for instance, you might not hear an approaching car!
I-Spy for 5 ☐

microphones
Just as a loudspeaker converts an electric signal to sound, a microphone does just the opposite. It converts sound to an electric signal, which is needed to make a recording.
I-Spy for 5 ☐

mixing console
A mixing console allows the recording engineer to control the balance of each 'track' (which contains the sound from each microphone). Many tracks are often necessary in producing a record, especially in orchestral and rock music.
I-Spy for 15 ☐

personal computer
The PC has eliminated a lot of bulky equipment which used to be necessary in the recording industry. It has also increased the degree of precision in controlling all parts of the recording and editing process.
I-Spy for 5 ☐

Pope St Gregory

Pope St Gregory (AD 540–604) is credited with being one of the founders of Western music. He organized a body of music called Gregorian Chant for use in the church.

I-Spy for 15 ☐

Palestrina

Giovanni Pierluigi Palestrina (1525–94) was perhaps the greatest composer of an age in which all significant music was written for the church. He wrote vocal music and was an unequalled master of counterpoint: a technique in which the voices weave in and out of each other.

I-Spy for 10 ☐

Monteverdi

Claudio Monteverdi (1567–1643) was one of the first composers of the Renaissance to establish a firm musical tradition outside the church. He was the first great composer of opera, but he also developed a range of other musical styles.

I-Spy for 10 ☐

Bach

Johann Sebastian Bach (1685–1750) was the most important figure of the Baroque period, and the greatest composer ever to write for the organ. His easier works are played even by beginners, but the counterpoint of his harder works is unsurpassed in its complexity.
I-Spy for 5 ☐

Haydn

Franz Joseph Haydn (1732–1809) was one of the greatest composers of the Classical period. Like other composers of his age, he wrote in a simpler style than Baroque composers. He is known as being the father of the symphony and of the string quartet.
I-Spy for 5 ☐

Mozart

Wolfgang Amadeus Mozart (1756–91) was another of the greatest composers of the Classical period. His works are blessed with beautiful and graceful melody. In his own lifetime he was not recognized as a true genius, and he died in poverty at the age of only 35.
I-Spy for 5 ☐

Beethoven

Ludwig van Beethoven (1770–1827) was the first man to force the world to accept that composers are artists of genius and not just tradesmen. His music is revolutionary and it led the way towards the Romantic period. Although he became deaf at about the age of 30, many of his greatest works were written after this.

I-Spy for 5 ☐

Brahms

Johannes Brahms (1833–97) was a great composer of the Romantic period. In contrast to Wagner, his works are quite conservative, because he felt strongly about preserving the traditions of the past.

I-Spy for 5 ☐

Wagner

Richard Wagner (1813–83) was one of the most influential men of the Romantic period and one of the greatest composers ever to write opera. He wanted to unify music and the other arts in his music dramas, which sometimes last more than four hours!

I-Spy for 5 ☐

Schoenberg

Arnold Schoenberg (1874–1951) was one of the first modern composers. He was the first to write atonal music (that is, music which is not based on a specific key). He invented a system of composition called 'serialism', which has been used by many twentieth-century composers.

I-Spy for 10 ☐

Stravinsky

Igor Stravinsky (1882–1971), along with Schoenberg, was the greatest composer of the first half of the twentieth century. He wrote in many styles, but he is probably best known for his early ballet works, such as *The Firebird*.

I-Spy for 10 ☐

Elgar

Edward Elgar (1857–1934) was England's finest Romantic composer. His marches are particularly famous, such as *Pomp and Circumstance*, but he is perhaps at his most powerful in intimate works like the Cello Concerto.

I-Spy for 5 ☐

Britten

Benjamin Britten (1913–1976) was the greatest modern English composer. He was primarily a vocal composer: he wrote many operatic masterpieces and dedicated a large number of his works to his close friend, the tenor Peter Pears.
I-Spy for **10**   ☐

Bernstein

Leonard Bernstein (1918–1990) left his mark as composer and as conductor. His pieces are strongly American in flavour, such as his famous *West Side Story*. As a great conductor he was known for his passionate performances, especially of Romantic music.
I-Spy for **5**   ☐

Rattle

Simon Rattle (1955–) is one of the greatest conductors of today. He has built a strong reputation with the City of Birmingham Symphony Orchestra and has done much to promote new music.
I-Spy for **5**   ☐

Davies

Peter Maxwell Davies (1934–) is probably the greatest living British composer. He has worked in a variety of styles. His complex early works have given way to a simpler melodic style since he moved to the Orkney Islands in the 1970s.

I-Spy for 10

Kennedy

Nigel Kennedy (1956–) is Britain's most famous active violinist. He has made an image for himself as a 'bad boy', breaking the unwritten rules of the musical establishment. He is interested in jazz and pop music as well as in classical music.

I-Spy for 5

du Pré

Jacqueline du Pré (1945–87) was one of Britain's finest cellists. She is known particularly for her recording of the Elgar Cello Concerto and her work with her husband, the conductor/pianist Daniel Barenboim. She died at an early age from multiple sclerosis.

I-Spy for 5

Joplin

Scott Joplin (1868–1917) was largely responsible for establishing a kind of popular music called 'ragtime' (possibly 'ragged time'). His most famous pieces are the 'Maple Leaf Rag' and the 'Entertainer'.

I-Spy 5 for hearing a
Scott Joplin piece ☐

Johnson

Robert Johnson (1911–38) is known as the father of the blues. He was a guitarist (before the days of the electric guitar), and many of his songs were later taken by other musicians, such as Eric Clapton. In his own day he was largely unrecognized.

I-Spy 15 for hearing a
Robert Johnson piece ☐

Armstrong

Louis Armstrong (1901–71), nicknamed 'Satchmo', started his career as a jazz trumpeter, but he later became more famous as a singer. His scratchy voice is unmistakable.

I-Spy 5 for hearing a
Louis Armstrong piece ☐

Parker

Charlie Parker (1920–55), who was known as the 'Bird', was one of the greatest saxophonists ever. He developed a style of jazz known as 'be-bop', which is noted for its very quick tempos and complex melodies.
I-Spy 5 for hearing a Charlie Parker piece ☐

Davis

The trumpeter Miles Davis (1926–91) has been a leading force in the development of jazz since the 1950s. He believed greatly in spontaneity, and his most famous album *Kind of Blue* (1959) was recorded mostly in one session. In later years he started the 'Fusion' movement, in which elements of jazz and rock are combined.
I-Spy 5 for hearing a Miles Davis piece ☐

Ellington

Duke Ellington (1899–1974) was one of the greatest jazz pianists of all time. He is most famous for his work with his big band, but he also made many recordings in smaller jazz combos. Many of the most famous standard tunes were written by him, such as 'Take the "A" Train'.
I-Spy 5 for hearing a Duke Ellington piece ☐

Clapton

Eric Clapton (1945–) is one of the most talented blues guitarists alive today. He was largely responsible for the blues revival in England during the 1960s. Today he continues the work he started 30 years ago.
I-Spy for 5 ☐

Berry

Known as the father of rock 'n' roll, Chuck Berry (1926–) was one of the first musicians to take up the electric guitar. For his day he had a very flamboyant playing style which was copied by many later rock guitarists.
I-Spy for 10 ☐

Elvis

Elvis Presley (1935–77), named the 'King of Rock 'n' Roll', did more than anyone else to bring the musical traditions of black America to a white audience. He was hugely popular.
I-Spy for 5 ☐

Beatles

The Beatles (1960–70), nicknamed the 'Fab Four', consisted of John Lennon, Paul McCartney, George Harrison, and Ringo Starr. They were perhaps the most successful band of all time before they broke up when Lennon left the group.
I-Spy for 5 ☐

Stones

The Rolling Stones (formed 1962), led by Mick Jagger, have endured amazingly for over 30 years. They were originally clean-cut musicians, but they soon led the way towards a more down-to-earth image for rock bands.
I-Spy for **5** ☐

Hendrix

The 'wild man' of 1960s rock, Jimi Hendrix (1942–70) stunned audiences with his guitar playing when he first arrived in England. He was the first musician to explore the full potential of the electric guitar. His playing and recordings are even more noteworthy considering the limited technology of his era.
I-Spy for **5** ☐

Floyd

Pink Floyd (formed 1965) was one of the first bands to make full use of the technology of the 1970s. In their albums, such as *The Wall* (1979), you can hear many special and complicated effects, mostly using only simple equipment.
I-Spy for **5** ☐

Gabriel

Peter Gabriel (1950–) has made the most of the technological advances of the 1980s. His albums take advantage of digital synthesizers and other special effects using digital technology. He has also used the music of other cultures in his own work.
I-Spy for **5** ☐

INDEX

© I-Spy Limited 1996

ISBN 1 85671 173 0

Michelin Tyre Public Limited Company
Edward Hyde Building, 38 Clarendon Road, Watford,
Herts WD1 1SX

MICHELIN and the Michelin Man are Registered
Trademarks of Michelin

A CIP record for this title is available from the British
Library.

Edited by Neil Curtis. Designed by Richard Garratt.

The Publisher gratefully acknowledges the contribution of
Performing Arts Library who provided the majority of the
photographs in this book. Additional photographs
courtesy of: Albert's Music Shop, Guildford; Bate
Collection, Faculty of Music, University of Oxford; Mary
Evans Picture Library; Richard Garratt; Jerry and Nick,
The Music Shop, Godalming; Redferns Music Picture
Library; A M Wright Esq., Merrow, Guildford; Yamaha-
Kemble Music. The Publisher also wishes to thank Tallis
Barker who compiled the text.

Colour reproduction by Anglia Colour Ltd.

Printed in Spain by Graficromo SA.